PAUL RUFFIN
NEW AND SELECTED POEMS

FOR AMBER

PAUL RUFFIN
NEW AND SELECTED POEMS

TCU PRESS
FORT WORTH, TEXAS

TCU TEXAS POETS LAUREATE SERIES

Library of Congress Cataloging-in-Publication Data

Ruffin, Paul.
  [Poems. Selections]
  New and selected poems / Paul Ruffin.
     p. cm. -- (TCU Texas poet laureate series)
  ISBN 978-0-87565-409-6 (alk. paper)
  1. Title.

PS3568.U362N49 2010
811'.54--dc22

                          2009033446

TCU Press
P. O. Box 298300
Fort Worth, Texas 76129
817.257.7822
http://www.prs.tcu.edu

To order books: 800.826.8911

Designed by fusion29
www.fusion29.com

This book is made possible by a generous Vision in Action grant from TCU.

TABLE OF CONTENTS

(continues)

(continues)

introduction

Paul Ruffin is Texas State University System Regents' Professor, Distinguished
Professor of English at Sam Houston State University, and the 2009 Texas State Poet
Laureate. In addition, he is a well-known author, not well-known as in a finalist on
American Idol, but known to those who read literary journals or mid-list popular books.

Even if he were not a writer, he would be a name among editors, with
The Texas Review, a literary magazine, and with The Texas Review Press. The press
sponsors four real-deal competitions that result in publication: George Garrett
Fiction Prize, Clay Reynolds Novella Prize, X. J. Kennedy Poetry Prize, and Robert
Phillips Poetry Chapbook Prize.

Occasionally, someone I know, maybe a student, becomes interested in
the publication game. After throwing out that perhaps he or she should find a
pursuit more likely to return cash to his or her pocket, I recommend sending off
fiction or non-fiction to *The Texas Review*. I do this because Sam Houston State
University's literary magazine consistently does a better job of introducing new
talent, going beyond publishing friends or making do with culls from established
writers. My students' work often strikes me as not particularly hot, but who am I to
say? Given this, I'm not sure if Ruffin and his staff appreciate me recommending
his lit journal.

A remarkable contribution to regional literature is *The Texas Anthology*,
which Ruffin edited in 1982. The compilation includes Vassar Miller, Pat LittleDog,
and Jack Myers, way back when. Ruffin also co-edited with George Garrett the 1993
anthology, *That's What I Like (About the South)*.

In terms of Ruffin's own writings, he is prolific. It is astounding how he
has done the editorial overseeing and class loads and still has found time to
publish—not written—publish, over a thousand poems, short stories, novels, and

nonfiction pieces. Forget the decades of unfailing artistry here. Think of the postal expense of that many SASEs.

I'll add that if you see Paul Ruffin's literary abilities in this book, but you are more of a prose person, I can recommend his short story collections, *The Man Who Would Be God, Islands, Women, and God* as well as *Jesus in the Mist.* That's correct. Two Gods and one Jesus. Most of Ruffin's prose and poetry, at least, hints at metaphysics.

I had already read Ruffin's book-length collections of poetry. I certainly enjoyed rereading the reprints in this TCU Press manuscript. It was fun to revisit such fine poems as "Cleaning the Well," "Circling," "When We Heard the Learned Astronomer Explain," and "The Animal at the Zoo Speaks of His Keeper."

I have long admired Ruffin's use of poetic devices. In "The Female Cousins Teach a Thanksgiving Lesson," in which an obnoxious boy gets his, Ruffin's alliteration and other sounds effectively finish off the poem:

> But Bobby huddles in his bed, winces
> at their cries, forlorn and shamed and shaken.

In "Returning to Luxapalila," the poet describes the bottom of a river as "the spongy primordial end of the world."

Another example of why his poetry should be read aloud is "Lighting the Furnace Pilot" It begins:

> Cold must come hard to our hill
> these winter nights, drive my wife
> to wool, her mood to ice,
> before I will climb to the attic
> to light the furnace pilot.

These lines are typical of Ruffin's subtle textured sounds: nice assonance in line three. The stanza is likeably conversational while full of crafted sound patterns.

It helps if you catch the allusions to Whitman, Yeats, and Lennon and McCarthy. But the true power of this book comes from its storytelling. This is most true in the last section of new poems. These lines from "Larry the Lawn Chair Man" will serve as an example:

> On a day in his San Pedro backyard,
>
> far from the classical world he yearned for,
>
> he sat strapped in a Sears lawn chair,
>
> forty-two weather balloons straining to lift him.

In "When the Mummy Became a Mommy," Ruffin coins the word "Necrafiligumbo" to develop that whimsical narrative. I'll let you read it to attain context. With the new material, readers will encounter compelling, often drop-dead funny story-telling. Ruffin has spent a meaningful part of his life in Mississippi, so the storytelling part is easy to explain.

Readers will find Paul Ruffin's inspired work in this fifth volume of the TCU Texas Poet Laureate Series. Enjoy Ruffin's inspirations. Enjoy this, the best of his hard work.

Billy Bob Hill
Editor, The TCU Texas Poets Laureate Series

I.
Poems from *Lighting the Furnace Pilot* (1980)

LIGHTING THE FURNACE PILOT

Cold must come hard to our hill
these winter nights, drive my wife
to wool, her mood to ice,
before I will climb to the attic
to light the furnace pilot.
There are no skeletons in my loft,
no pulsing bats. A firm mind
and wire mesh keep them out
with the early frost and ruined leaves—
it is neither fate nor fear.

My ascension creaks the ladder
and I slide back the panel and
hoist my extra twenty pounds
up among the rafters.
No bats, or bones, I think,
my fingers finding the knob
that will put breath back
into this winter house.
Then the blue jet sings,
fire pops from a hundred holes
as I hunker in the dark and warm,
my hands on the furnace sides.
Above my head the leaves
flit and finger across the roof,
and the wind, heavier and a year
older, moans from fate or fear.

cleaning the well

Each spring there was the well to be cleaned.
On a day my grandfather would say,
"It's got to be done. Let's go." This time
I dropped bat and glove, submitted to the rope,
and he lowered me into the dark and cold
water of the well. The sun
slid off at a crazy cant and I was
in icy water, grappling for whatever
was not pure and wet and cold.

The sky hovered like some pale moon
above, eclipsed by his heavy red face
bellowing down to me not to dally,
to feel deep and load the bucket.
My feet rasped against cold stone,
toes selecting unnatural shapes, curling
and gripping, raising them to my fingers,
then into the bucket and up to him:
a rubber ball, pine cones, leather glove,
beer can, fruit jars, an indefinable bone.
It was a time of fears: suppose he
should die or forget me, the rope break,
the water rise, a snake strike, the
bottom give way, the slick sides crumble?

The last bucket filled, my grandfather
assured, the rope loop dropped to me
and I was delivered by him who
sent me down, drawn slowly to sun
and sky and his fiercely grinning face.
"There was something else down there:
a cat or possum skeleton, but it
broke up, I couldn't pick it up."

(continues)

He dropped his yellow hand on my head.
"There's always something down there
you can't quite get in your hands.
You'd know that if it wasn't your first
trip down. You'll know from now on."

"But what about the water?
Can we keep on drinking it?"

"You've drunk all that cat
you're likely to drink. Forget it,
and don't tell the others. It's just
one more secret you got to live with."

Deep-Sea Fishing

In farm ponds or rivers
there is always the bottom
to be felt, something at the end
of your paddle or pole
to tell you the earth is there.
And the longest gar is less
than the length of your leg.
Fish with two eyes, one on a side,
look right, even in air, scales
or skin familiar as freckles.

But here the terrible fish feed deep,
huddling around sand-choked ships,
whatever lies below: pipelines, abandoned nets,
the one-eyed, grotesque, colors
and shapes of another world.
Here hauling in a taken line
is done with care, a club
close by, a sharp knife
to cut the singing line.
The cottonmouth, the thunder-
jawed loggerhead, the sharp-
toothed gar are petty thoughts
here where the fish feed deep
and silent and their unknown forms
run deep behind the eyes.

It is like the fear of falling,
here where the earth fails us.
And even when the old known sun
has flattened out the sea
like a hammer on lead,
as the line goes slicing,
fingers tighten on the rod,
eyes tighten on the sea,
the deep, dark green of the sea.

CALF IN AN ABANDONED WELL

For Marsha

Once more those images storm my mind
this day of sun and easy air,
once more black wings spiral down,
whoom to a stop beside the hole.
And dark settles on the land, chokes
the summer hill wind, stills the eyes
like farm ponds before the blackness breaks.

The shaping of an afternoon is slow.
The pines opened like a wound
and then the well was there, around
it dark birds, horny heads
bobbing, the shuffling mass whirling
like pagans in some fierce dance.
They broke in a clap of bright black,
rose into the trees, arching them
with dark wind, and the calf
belly glowed from the well bottom,
pinioned by a shaft of stench.

The years have driven us our ways,
bright hours and dark, your letters coming
fewer, less often, saying less, lost
deep in whatever wounds we have left.
I cannot say what ties us yet,
perhaps nothing, perhaps the tenuous
clutch we still have, the sense of black,
unfathomable black: well and wing,
the sag of a summer afternoon
into Orphic loss, some dark wind.

HOTEL FIRE: NEW ORLEANS

From first light we fear falling:
after the fever of birth, impetus
toward that natural window, we
reach, cling, our fingers and toes
curled to grip, after the fire
that tempers us for the sun.

There I saw them—I see them still—
thrust from windows,
flailing like children
who know the earth has failed them:
they snatch at chinks, cling to ledges,
tumble to the wet street below,
the fire an old and certain death,
the leap the only faith that's left.

After the Fire at the Old Folks Home

Deep in this smoke-choked night
they line the armory hall
like frightened children: clutching
a purse here, a blanket there,
pictures and paper sacks.
The shock-stained faces so soon
jarred from sleep hold the long stare
of dream, the slow motion of dream.
Fingers tighten whitely on the
few salvaged scraps of lives
while we wipe away smudges
and bandage what bleeds or burns.
And then we leave them, dumb
to say it will be better tomorrow,
the sun will come, the night go.
What child or bird could rise
renewed with bright eyes shining
after such an ashy death,
so fierce a night of burning?

TO a STUDENT on THE FRONT ROW

For Leeanne Harriman, MSU, 1972

Children may someday pick
up your bones, a late April,
from the secret earth,
feel your fingers the way
I roll this piece of chalk,
pelvic bone scrubbed clean
of mud and moss, turned up
on a log, the girlflesh gone, the bright
hair, that bleached chamber hollow
to the rattle of stones they toss.
Your smooth thigh bones,
in their hot hands, will
bludgeon frogs and snakes,
and teeth I have dreamed against
mine will be parceled out
among small pockets to
clack with marbles and rocks.

On the front row, on the front
your hair lies across your
shoulders, soft and warm
in a yellow rib of sun.

TO PATSY: TENTH GRADE

You were as common, those days,
Patsy, as a squat milk jug,
dress tugged to cover your ankles,
lipstick as taboo as beer,
and so swollen on Christ
we took your word when
you said He was your lover.

But when Vandevender took you
back there behind the gym
in those tall dark weeds
and you gave up the ghost,
your resurrected bones
turned the world round for us
who saw you rise from damp rushes
that night like a silver chalice
rubbed bright by the Master's hands.

Pompeii

The ruins of Pompeii, 1969

In the glare of the day the tragic
shape will not come: colorful
tourists clatter about the streets
and the ruins reflect civic
concern: the high polish of trade.
The ash has been scooped, buried,
blown away to bare this bright
place to common air, the sun,
and busy prying hands and eyes.
Ah, the tragedy lacks its starch,
wilts in this bustle and chatter.

Here on the night slopes of Vesuvius
the tragic tale begins: Pompeii
rises from the ash-dark plain, the moon
coaxes inch by inch walls and columns.
Dogs bark, the earth moves,
bent and broken rise and walk,
the scorched, the stifled—all
bright and whole in the moon's healing.

But the sun wakes what the moon dreams.
Its first slashes bring the color back,
vehicles move, a slow string of early
tourists inches toward the town.
The ghosts are gone, the tragedy still.
Polished ruins sit waiting
vacant on the dawning plain.

THE PRACTICE IS OVER, TOM HARDY

When you are turned this time
from your worm-drilled coffins, ghosts,
it will not be the thump of guns,
the firefly practice on the coast.

The shudder that shakes
the Salisbury Plain,
the hot press of shock,
will spare the glebe cow pain
and instant-fleece the flock,
leaving a sooty shadow
where the hound had lain.

It will be warmer then indeed:
the Judgment will be known at last,
when Stourton Tower poofs like Camelot
and Stonehenge melts like glass.

TO THE TWENTY-FIRST CENTURY

Blue-clad boy
asleep under the haystack
or lost in the corn,
drag out and blow again
your old and tarnished horn,
now that the cows have bloated
and the sheep run wild.
Blow it again,
now that the order we held
as fine-balanced and fragile
as a house of straw
has tumbled to the wind.
Blow it again, you first
notion that order does not last,
blue innocent in a book
of color and rhymes where
there is no future nor past.
Up and blow, boy, blow to
the skies, but know that your
tune is lost on casual green and blue.
As you wish, stand and blow,
though bronze to iron to atom
to dreamless sleep is the way
that this story will go.

Trimming a Tree at Forty

Not understanding fully the facts
of gravity and old bones,
when Miss Johnson, eighty if a day,
tumbled down the steps of the church
and broke her hip, we kids asked why
she did not get up and walk, the way
we would have done. She trembled on
the lowest step, a fistful of liver.
The ambulance and pale faces, the
chalky whispers that day were
our mystery, darkening
into weeks before she died.

Today I clung twenty feet
from the ground to limbs
I would have squirreled across then:
I inched and clasped, arms and legs,
the earth so far away my breath
burned with the fear of falling.
Pride kept me up there,
the pile of limbs sprawling below
into the shape of an old woman
hard against the ground; the chalk-
dry wind whispered me down,
gravity swung on my bones.

THE HIGH SCHOOL ENGLISH TEACHER RETIRES

For thirty-five years she did battle
against ignorance, that childhood evil:
nurtured the wise, subdued the rabble,
and wrestled with all the uncertainties
that obliterate the soul.

At sixty she simply wound down
like a dusty childless toy:
shelved her books, turned
once around in the chalky room
and tilted on home.

She says she is beyond hurt now,
even the recent wounds do not matter
at this age, and the old ones
lie smooth as frozen lakes at dawn.

.

II.
Poems from *Circling* (1996)

JODY WALKER: THE FIRST VOICE

Jody—the name conjures fawn and fowl,
the smack of scuppernong wine.

Strung in a row, we lolled each
morning, waiting for his bus
to reach school, our tongues
and fingers sharp to touch
what he delivered: blackberries
silver with dew and big as cows' eyes,
possum on a chain, ratsnake
around his neck, pickled
pig embryo, rubbers with spikes,
wines rendered from the wildest fruits,
the stuffed two-headed calf
John Parker threw up over,
owl eggs, flying squirrels,
dried bull balls black as coal—
his store of exotics as endless
as the earth itself.

Shorter by a head than most of us,
he had merely to wink, gesture,
cup a palm toward us, and we
followed, older, younger, where he led.
He charmed us with tales
of coupling animals, showed us
how babies came to be, shared
photographs of nudes, taught us
how farm boys drove deep
into the soft of fruit and beasts.

His was our brightest sin:
Our dwarf god from out
as far as the buses could go
stepped down from his yellow
chariot, his hand beckoning.
His secrets burned in us.
Each morning we grew in his flame
beneath that simple sun.

Frozen over

In Mississippi I recall only once
how the cold came down like a lid of iron,
clamping the landscape, stilling the trees,
and all the ponds froze over: not
just a skim for crashing rocks through,
but thick and hard enough to walk on.
The gravel pit where we swam in summer
spanged and creaked as I edged out
toward the gray, awful middle where,
if I went through, no one could reach.

I moved like a bird coming to terms
with glass, sliding one foot, then
the other, holding back my weight
and breath until they had to come.

I could see, beyond the far shore,
cars moving on the highway, slowing,
faces in the window ringed with frost,
the little ones waving, pointing
to that child walking on water.

CIrCLInG

A lesson learned while coon hunting

"When you are lost in night woods,"
my father said, pointing about us,
"you can't just guess at a line:
one leg's shorter, you'll circle.
You must walk in a set direction,
picking a tree, one farther on,
and on, until you have strung out
tree after tree in a straight line
to some place better than where you are."

"But in the dark?" I questioned him.

"There's always enough light for that,
but don't you trust the stars and moon—
they move." He asked if I understood.
I nodded and looked at the dark trees.

"Then find your way back to the truck."

"But it's getting late, I'm hungry,
I don't know what direction to start."

"That is the direction. Now *go!*"
He pointed to the wall of woods.

I lunged into the underbrush
in the direction he had pointed,
forgetting utterly his advice,
no tree different from another,
crashed and plunged until I knew
that I was lost and circling.
I could see nothing but dark trees,
hear nothing but my terrified run
and the thrashing of my heart.
The stars spun wildly overhead,
the moon bounced across the sky.

(continues)

He let me wander, stumbling, calling
his name until the woods stilled
and I crouched, wet and cold,
like some wild abandoned thing
waiting for him to find me.

"You did not pick a tree," he said
as I followed him out of the woods,
"you did not hold a direction."

I stepped in his moon-cast shadow,
long leg, short leg, resisting the circle
until the stars fell into place
and the rising moon stood still.

GIGGING FROGS

There are some things on this earth
that may be fooled by two moons,
one still as a stone in the sky,
the other dancing. Not these frogs.
A moonlit night is not a night
for going after frogs. When your light
joins the moon, their clatter stops,
the pond goes dead: they are not fooled.

It must be done on a dark and dooming night
when yours will be the only light above
the rim of the pond. You must move
with the stealth of winter with your moon,
as slow as a stone sliding across the sky.
Then, as you see the eyes take life in
a seeming joy, moonstruck, you steady
the light, aim the deadly gig, and jab
the prongs through belly or head,
swift and sure as a cottonmouth.

When you have taken all you want, you
must ice them down for the trip home,
first cutting the hind legs, still joined,
from the upper torso, skinning them
like removing too-tight jeans
and laying them side by side
in the ice of your cooler,
the legs of so many lovely girls
collected by a moonstruck man
who slew them for his joy.

BaTTInG ROCKS

It is lonesome, like something lost,
this twist of body to send a rock sailing
from the slap of a piece of oak flooring.
Long-unused muscles try to remember,
eye unsure, the stance experimental.
But I will fill this pasture, marked
for a baseball field, with liners and flies,
homeruns beyond the calfpen and barn.

Switching from right to left, I can
almost remember the boy I was, squared
in the gravel road before my father's
house, batting the lingering day away,
can almost recall the rosters I kept,
with names like Mantle, Berra, and Mays,
can know again the whir of a foul, crack
of a long drive into the deep fields
beyond my nearest neighbor's yard.
Now, with my cows looking on like annoyed
neighbors and the light failing fast, I
toss up another rock, set to swing, then
bring the oak slat across in a level arc.
Wood and stone connect and the rock sails
high and away, beyond the peak of the barn.

It is a homerun, and I am satisfied. I
stand quiet and watch Berra, his short
legs churning, rounding third for home.

BUryInG

I found him stumbling about when the mother
died, an otherwise healthy calf, and fed him
by bottle until another cow came due, then
moved him in with her for suckling.
Third night she broke his neck.
It was a right and natural thing to do:
She reasoned her milk was for hers alone.
I found him barely breathing, head thrown
back, unable to rise for the bottle,
his eyes already hazing over. I could see
myself fading in them, backing into fog.
I brought the pipe down hard, twice, the
second time in malice: not for him or her,
but for the simple nature of things.
Blood came from his nose, his body
quivered. I dragged him from the barn.

The hole in the winter garden was easy, quick,
and the calf fit properly, but when the
first shovel of dirt struck his side,
he kicked, with vigor. I watched the flailing
foot strike against air. Nothing else moved.
There were no considerations: I did what
needed to be done. A few more scoops clamped
the leg and the earth stilled. I mounded
the grave and turned away, looking back once
to see that nothing heaved. I felt neither
fear nor sorrow, love nor hate. I felt
the slick handle of the shovel, slid
my thumb over its bright steel blade,
breathed deep the sharp and necessary air.

SAWDUST PILE

A pile, they say,
will burn for twenty years,
seething with deep heat
those long years out,
cool enough on top
for weeds and barefoot boys.

Like early ice it lures
the unwary up a greening slope
firm to the foot, firm
and cool up to the very peak,
where the crust sags, gives way,
and legs, torso, and head
sink to the fierce core.

There are the tales:
Bo Simpson's horse, a pack
of pure-blood coon hounds,
Sarah Potter's little girl
all gone to a quick hell.

Out here the rattler warns, lightning
strikes from a growling sky:
each terror is given a tongue.
But the fire lies quiet in this pile,
a coiled thing, tongueless and waiting,
beneath the devil's cool shell.

LLano Estacado: The Naming

When Coronado and his three hundred
soldiers and six hundred Pueblo slaves
pursued El Turco across this grand plateau,
he could not have known what he had entered
until mile after trackless mile they followed
their phantom prey and found on all sides
the same stretch of grass and sky,
only at night orienting themselves, gazing
at the same constellations they had known
before their ascent into a shadeless hell.

In this land of alkaline waters, broken
by sudden ravines that yawned hotly open
as if the earth would swallow them,
the plated soldiers rode, sweltering
in the merciless sun, the shimmering air.
Some fell, clattering, never to rise again,
some threw their armor aside and faced the sun.

Behind them, where nearly a thousand had passed,
the grass closed like water and all about them
was nothing but the sameness of the grassy sea.
So in time they came to cut from stunted trees
that lined dry washes poles to mark their way.
Mile after mile they drove the sticks
as they moved, stakes that leaned in the wind,
trailing out behind them, monuments to their folly,
telling them nothing of where they were going
and little of where they had been.

DrouGHT

The storms build from noon,
flatten on top and darken
into great bears roaring across
summer, dormancy over, the
rumble of appetite everywhere.

My hoe clatters in the dust,
the blade turning up clouds
of white powder that pales
the bent and punished beans.
My chest burns with dust
while the bears grumble
and rear, hovering over me,
waving their windy arms.
They mutter off to other places.

I curse them, shaking my hoe,
daring them as they weaken
and hang in the distance
like healing bruises,
then turn back to my rows,
where even briars and thistle
must strike their roots deep
into hardpan, their tops leathery,
chastised by long days of sun.

The bears will not rise again
until late tomorrow in this
land of the dry bones.
Beginning at noon, my eyes
will roll like knuckles toward
the sky, daring them to come.
The sun banks low, the western sky
clearing for another dewless night.
The land stretches a long dry yawn.

ROOT-Pruning

*Root-pruning is a horticultural procedure consisting of
digging a shallow trench around the base of a fruit tree,
severing feeder roots and traumatizing the tree into
fruition.*

The shock of my shovel
trembles through you
like some loud clanging
at the gates, the
distant rattle of swords.
Yet this must be done
if your dullness is to break
and the fruit come.

I feel the blade stop,
gather strength, slice through
roots as thin as veins
matted on a lover's lids.

There is no love in this:
It is not a gentle procedure.
I can see in your barren limbs
against the sky that awful need
begin, the primal racial fear:
that blessed rage for seed.

THE STORM CELLAR

For Walt McDonald

Those green summer afternoons
when writhing fingers dance
across the Texas plains
my family will huddle here.

We gave up an apple tree and pear
to have this maw of concrete and steel—
It waits obscenely, its raw
back a gray hump on the lawn.

When green waves of wind fling
against the ribs of our house
and dash the heavens down,
our fate will lie in that damp belly
where we will be swallowed and saved
for a brighter day: thrown up
weak and short of breath, wet
with fear, but glad of this gray beast
and what is left to be counted and kept.

winter trout

The Pascagoula River, December 1997

It is like other rivers you've known,
sliding off to somewhere, except that
here you can see where it has been going.
To the south it flattens out to green
Gulf that curls to the edge of the sky.
In the summer what takes your bait
may be bass or bream or catfish, teetering
at the edge of fresh water and brine,
moving upstream and down as rains come
and flush the channel, tilt the balance.

But now it is winter, and the trout have come
from their salty summer around the islands
to spawn and feed and wait for spring rains.
You troll the river and adjoining lakes
until your reel sings that a trout has struck.
Then you anchor and fish the school until
they move off or stop striking. The hunt
begins again, in this place of confused waters,
where the summer fish run with the winter fish
and the river meets the sea.

REDFISH

Sometimes, when they move in schools,
you can see them out from the beach
inching like a ghost along the gullies,
a shapeless red blob, no fish distinct
from another, a vague smear like blood.
The secret is to cast in front of them
and drag a flashing lure through the mass.

Then the fight to the beach begins,
you with one eye on your arching rod,
the other on the disappearing school,
your mind torn between what you have
and the ghost just out of your reach.

But it is no time for philosophy.
Your body takes over, stomach firms
the rod butt, left hand a fulcrum
that balances you and him, right
a furious crank that wills him
a loop at a time to you, who
at the moment must settle
for what you know is real.

WHEN WE HEARD THE LEARNED ASTRONOMER EXPLAIN THE THEORY OF THE EXPLODING UNIVERSE

With gratitude to Dr. Frank Drake

He could have explained it in
a technical way, cold, exact:
velocities, trajectories, white dwarfs,
red giants and black holes,
a man who knows nothing but stars,
or warmed us with a metaphor:
"The shrapnel of our exploding celestial
shell will fling on forever out
until nothing will be left
except the sense of burst and bang,"
his eyes aglitter with something
like joy, scientist with a grin,
cocking his head and clucking at us
like a proud, successful hen.

Instead we sat and heard him tell
his story as if he aimed it at
the sleeping child on my shoulder,
like some sad-eyed boy with a truth
that we all should have known:
"The best way I can tell you this
is all the bright stars will be gone."

Fever

For two days and a night
our daughter has slept with that hot angel,
cool rags and aspirin doing little
to set her system right.
She heaves against the weight
that presses her to the bed—
it is almost love, you've said,
watching her body burn and twist.

She moans in sleep, mumbles
with whatever ghost she dreams,
and when sun brightens her room
her face is fierce and numb
to our touch, her hot eyes
looking through or around us
who cannot see the incubus
that will not let her rise.

DRESSING UP

It will not do to say to her,
Child, the time will come for all this.
It is better to watch from another room
as she smears on lipstick and rouge
before the mirror by her bed,
lost in her mother's summer dress,
gloves and high heels and hat,
swallowed by what she will grow into.

But that, we say, *is all right,* as if
there were more that we could do or say.
We are merely here to feed her dreams
and see that they are pleasing
until she awakes, a strange face
in a mirror beside some other bed,
with lace and gloves, hat and shoes
of her own shape and of her choosing.

MY SON AT COMMUNION

My son, age five, is perplexed
by the wafers and the wine his sister takes
and will not be instructed on symbols,
preferring in his literalist mind to think
of matters of the body, not the soul.

A Sunday morning I find him
crouched in a sunny corner of his room,
a shaft of light cleaving him like a sword,
in one hand a miniature Ritz cracker,
in the other a brandy glass of purple Welch.
"This is the body," he says, not knowing
I watch, "and this is the blood."
He slides the cracker onto his tongue and chews,
drains down the juice, wipes the lip
of the glass with his shirt sleeve.
He bows and whispers a prayer
as I back from the silent, holy room,
struck with the need to believe.

BUDDY PHILOSOPHIZES AFTER CUTTING
THE BULL

"You locate the seam along the middle
of the sack," Buddy says, pinching the calf's
scrotum for me to see, "and make a cut
just big enough for the nut on each side:
that way it don't bleed much and there ain't
much to heal." He makes the first cut,
squeezes out a bullet-like testicle, slices
it off, and moves to the other side.
The calf lunges, but our ropes hold.
Buddy throws the second testicle over the fence,
sprays disinfectant on the cuts. He frees
the calf and accepts another beer.
       "You don't
eat them?" I ask. He shakes his head no:
"It's lot that does, but not me."
       "Why not?"
"Well, that stuff comes from believin' that
eatin' somebody else's balls will make you
more potent, but Lord knows I don't need that.
If anything, I sometimes wish somebody'd make
some cuts on me. All we done was take the rage
out of him—no tearin' through fences, pacin'
and bellerin', all for one white-hot shot of fun."
He sighs and reaches for another bottle of beer.
"No sir, we'd all be better off without'm, balls—
instruments of torture and the baggage of fools."

SHUCKING OYSTERS, OR FISHING
FOR METAPHORS

My father-in-law goes at it for three hours,
gouging the horny lumps we've gathered:
the black crust splits to pearl—
"Storm breaking to a pearl sky," I think,
and the oyster lies there, a glob of mucous
in its own faint milk.

       "They're fat," he says.
It joins others in a green bowl. Shells
gather beside him.

       "The shells," I ask,
"what'll we do with the shells?"

"We have to put them back—each one has
an oyster germ, produces a new oyster."

"That's perpetual life," I muse,
and snoop around for oyster germs.
The bowl fills slowly, slowly.
"Hard go, isn't it?" I nod at the pile.

"Oh, it's not so bad, just a little slow."
His hands, dark and hard as the shells,
move with a learned precision: fishing
a lump, wedging the knife into a seam
so tight I cannot see it, prying
and scooping with one motion.
"Tight as a virgin's cleft," I say to myself.
"Not poetry, but damned close."
The shells clack onto the pile,
the bowl fills to the rim.

(continues)

"Any pearls?
Did you find any pearls among those?"

"No, not this time. Doesn't happen often,
sometimes one the size of a pin-head."
No pearls in those blear eyes. I remember
a Negro's dead eye, lumped in its milk,
but I prefer not to bring it up.

He lifts an oyster with the tip of his knife,
holds it on his tongue, then swallows.
He motions one to me; I take it
and gnash it down.

"It's like something
that ought to be coming up and out
instead of in and down," I suggest.

"Sauce makes it better, or lemon."
The shucking done, he sacks the shells,
I carry the bowl back to the house.
I am out of metaphors, he of oysters.
The sky tries to remind me of something
I want to be thinking about, the oysters slosh
in the bowl. The lawn, I think, needs rain.

EXPLAINING TO MY DAUGHTER HOW A POEM BEGINS

Do not be fooled, my little dear,
by these pretty things we're reading.
It is not enough that they look
like poems or sound like them —
though this is necessary and good.

You have asked about their origins.
Here is the mystery, the dark return to birth:
The poem rises out of us
like some shaggy thing that must be chained
and subdued to the useful and the good,
adapted to the light of day,
trimmed for the neighbor's eye,
its bellow refined to a song.

What lies warm and easy on the lap
and pleases us measure for measure,
begins with an urgency in the bowels
and wordless white-eyed terror.

THE SEINE

When the water drops and trickles,
settling into still, dark holes,
we unroll the twenty-foot seine
and lug it off to the river.

Strung between us, one at each end
to steady the poles and guide,
the seine bellies out and sweeps up
whatever cannot go over or under
or around our churning feet:
perch and bass and catfish,
sticks and rocks, turtles, snakes,
all that swims or lies in that low river.

After each drag we separate fish
from what we do not want
and move to another hole.
So it continues the day long
until we tire or the buckets
fill with minnows and fish.

With the seine strung from clotheslines
to dry, we crouch by a backyard fire
and clean the day's catch, rolling
a few pieces in cornmeal and throwing
them into a pot of roiling grease.

Later, our bellies full of fish and beer,
we watch the seine bow out and fill
with wind and catch the rising moon.

SHRIMPING

It is not so much the shrimp
that have brought me out here,
those flicking brown knuckles,
as the seething bag of life
we dump onto the picking board.

My father-in-law yanks the knot:
the pile—crabs, shrimp, sundry fish—
settles out across the board,
riding on its own silver slime
until as far as I can reach
the sea has spread its mystery.

We ease the net out again,
dropping lines and chains
to drag while we separate shrimp
from what will not be kept.
With spatula and fork we rake out
claw-waving crabs, flopping rays,
whatever could pinch or sting;
shrimp go into an ice chest.

My father-in-law identifies
the things I do not know, shapes
and colors odd in the sun,
creatures of another world
our sweeping net has gathered.
His hand avoids spines and teeth,
pulls one prize after another out,
holds them up for me to see.

(continues)

As the sun begins to settle down,
we pull the net a final time,
rinse it in the wake, and turn
for home, toward beginning lights.

We are slimed and stained, hair
aglitter with scales, our hands
pricked and burning from spines
and smeared with hot jellies of the sea.

We do not talk on our way back,
our minds on what we have
and what we have left. I tilt
my beer to the falling sun
and the dark water below.

III.
Poems from *The Book of Boys and Girls* (2003)

AT THE RUINS

On a blanket we made love
beside the ruins of the little cabin,
a sprawl of tin and rotted lumber,
that no woman ever entered.
For years it served us when
we scoured the river bottoms
for all that boys search for
before they discover women,
knowing them only
as distractions, a vague haunting.
First they find girls,
who are not women,
but what women come from:
perfect of form, wiggly and giggly
and sweet as woods in spring,
their bodies fumbled over later
in the back seats of cars,
on soiled mattresses
in huts and abandoned houses.
They must wait for women,
mothers and teachers and neighbors' wives,
who smell of chalk and kitchens,
wax and soap and bleach,
whose eyes no boy can fathom.
For women must be earned
and women must be learned.
When we are finished we stand
beside the cabin ruins, silent,
as if we gazed on moonlit Troy.
I pull her to me and cling
like a child, the smell of her
all moss and leaves and earth
and woman, woman, woman.

NaSTY NOTeS aT THe acaDemIc conFerence

SCMLA Conference, Biloxi, circa 1988

In this place of high seriousness
we giggle and rub feet beneath the table.
Somber scholars about us read
over papers they will present.
We are away from the children two days
and we are not thinking like scholars.

I take a napkin, fold it in half,
and write a proposition, slide
it over. She smiles and answers
and slides the napkin back.
We know where this is going
and what it will be like when we get there.
There will be no great surprises.

We are over the age of fiery
discovery in books and bodies
and care nothing for fad approaches:
Freudian or Marxist or feminist,
the one hundred new positions.
We are not into deconstruction.

Our note is a simple back and forth
of marital fun, and nothing more.
We finish our drinks and smile,
and I lead her by the hand
to the elevator, past those serious
heads nodding at their papers.
We will learn nothing new where we are going,
and deliver nothing new. Yet something
will tremble in the universe,
stars will flash and tumble,
in our small season suns will spin.
We will leave no mark here,
take nothing home to tell the others.
The doors close and we ascend.

Returning to the Luxapalila

The river is the color of earth, fed by runoff
from pastures and fields of cotton and corn
and forestland heavy with humus.
Kneeling by the water near a shale outcropping,
I shatter my face and settle my outspread hand,
palm up, until it fades from sight
like something drowned in history's dark pages—
now you see it, now you don't.
Watching the hand disappear, I see
the face of a girl eased down by the pastor,
her paleness and blond hair darkened,
held below that brown rush
until she broke the surface again,
arms flung wide in the flaring sun,
face shining like an angel's,
white marble with thin blue veins
trailing from her temples to blend
with water whispering off her hair,
dress sheer and tight on her tiny breasts,
Thank you, Jesus, he cried to the water and the woods.

Here as a boy I curled at the end
of a cable swing, flung out, released,
hung there, wingless creature floating on air
until gravity snatched me and I dropped
breathless to the river, the flash of green bank,
the sun a yellow something spinning on blue,
then my feet entering the water, my body
going down through that wet tunnel,
the color of weak whiskey across my eyes,
a darker stronger bourbon, then nothing,
slipping into the Earth itself, and deeper,
until my feet touched the bottom,
the spongy primordial end of the world.
A thrust and I rose through the tunnel,
eyes uplifted toward the brightness,
hands and arms battering like wings
to burst breathless to green and blue,

(continues)

the steady round face of the Sun,
my vision bleared by water,
the taste of earth upon my tongue.

My feet uncertain against the muddy slope,
I clamber back to the level of brush and briar
on the bluff, watch the brown ribbon below
weaving around a grassy bar, and see—
is it a simple slant of light
breaking from behind me?—
the girl's marble-white face rising free,
hair streaming, cupped by my hand,
her arms stretched out to the mounting sun.

TIIe MYSterY FOr THC MaGUS

The mystery for me was not the mewling child
nestled in cloth, above whose birthing room
I *think* a bright star hovered.
I was focused not on that simple stable —
where it was clear that something
of great note had happened
nor on the message whispered 'round
that Christ had come,
delivered without consummated love—
but on the woman, neck curved like a swan,
hair pulled back from her round, dark face
where tears of joy still had not dried,
whose eyes looked down on this baby
who had sprung from her inviolate body.

Chosen as a vessel of life as she always is,
woman, this woman, did not question how
the thing had happened, would not have cared
that the child before her might in his time
herd camels or fling nets for fish
or as a girl-child gather olives
or slave at making bread,
and nightly bear the weight of a man.

And were he to turn assassin or thief,
she would forgive even as *He* would
when He faced the world of men.
It was all the same to her:
a child is but a child,
engendered by swarthy beggar
or by device of God.
The love I witnessed there
was no more than I had seen elsewhere,
and the star in time I saw as any other
beneath which a woman beamed
upon what she had delivered,
wet with her blood and wearing
a divine glow, her eyes the first
and only heaven that child might ever know.

THE WOMAN WHO MADE LOVE ON
FROST'S GRAVE

With gratitude to Mrs. John Gardner for the story...

She made love once on Frost's grave—
the night after their marriage, her husband
with less knowledge of the man's words
than the silent earth he was buried in.

And did she take on some of his power,
back pressed hard against that stone cover,
his graven name burned between her shoulders,
did she glow in the darkness beneath her lover?

She would not say except through her wild eyes,
this woman vexed with a new-found strength
who, sandwiched between the living and dead,
had felt a feverish trembling to all her length.

THE FEMALE COUSINS TEACH A
THANKSGIVING LESSON

They have huddled their pretty heads
in the barn—raven hair and tawny.
Surfeited at last, they agree
that they will have no more
of this boy's vile and wicked ways,
his foul mouth and crude touching.

When females gather to address
a common threat upon them,
best the men pay heed and watch
the fate that might befall them.

Strutting down the path,
he stops and leans and listens.

"Oh, Bobby Wayne, Bobby Wayne,"
the voice comes from out the hedge,
smooth as panty silk and soft as summer butter,
"would you like to see me now
with all my clothes from off me
and feel my you-know-what, Sir?"

Possessed of less than common sense,
but blessed with hormones plenty,
he knows not the lessons of men
who shunned the wisdom of girls
and suffered lacerations many.

(continues)

Bobby enters boldly past the green
surface of the hedge like plunging into water
and finds himself enjungled there—
six sets of claws unsheathed, three mouths
howling, three racks of fangs upon him.

And when at last he frees himself
and crawls from out the cover,
Bobby is less the man he was,
a shocked and trembling thing,
weak and mewling like a baby,
young skin torn and bleeding now,
his pride stripped bare of what it was,
ravaged soul and body.

For days in his room he lies, or he sits sullen,
while outside his window dash the girls,
crying gaily, "Bobby, Bobby, catch us,
if you can, and you may have us.
We are but little Gypsy girls, harmless
as the wind and ripe now to be taken."

But Bobby huddles in his bed, winces
at their cries, forlorn and shamed and shaken.

THE ANIMAL AT THE ZOO SPEAKS
OF HIS KEEPER

Here I am sleek as an otter but not one,
my nose swept out, down, and up,
bulbed properly, and sharp in any wind.
My ears lie mostly flat against my head,
I raise them when I need to.
I cannot read the sign on the post
outside my cage that tells what I am.
I am what I am.

A man with foul breath and teeth
the color of my belly fur
dutifully brings my food and water
and daily cleans my cage.
I dine on fish and crunchy nuggets.

Days when the sun is right,
through the trees I can see
it dance far off on the bay,
but that light might well be
the flash of a distant star
for what it means to me.

Born here, what I remember
of sunlit shores and forage,
whizzing like a brown bullet
through glass-clear water
into schools of shattering fish,
I do not remember at all.
I cannot explain this.

(continues)

But the man who feeds me
might know. He has books.
Some days I see him reading
from a dark book on a bench
while he has his sandwich and drink.

I think he might be religious,
the book comforting to him.
Some days I see him looking
through the same trees toward
the dancing sunlight on the bay.

TO THE CELIBATE

It is your choice, and no one will fault you
for choosing as you have. But recall that
beyond the magnificence of your room,
your books and paintings,
glassware and rich mahogany,
the china bath with golden handles,
the color and light and sound
that rival all nature can offer,
beyond your burning dreams of this life,
your head filled with enormous learning,
beyond the riches of this cloister,
you are bone and flesh, designed to breed
and die, no less than the purest holy man,
no more than the lowly oyster.

NESTING

About her she has gathered pillows and blankets,
arranging them just so, then peopled her nest with dolls,
those with anatomies quite far from correct, glittering
eyes of glass, flesh very unlike her own, some merely
limp or plump, dimpled and dappled pieces of cloth
with dull fabric eyes and skin, no fingers or toes.

It seems to make no difference to her as she places
them about her in the ring, tucking each one in for the night,
the one with the rocking blue eyes shining in their sockets,
the one with round black patches where eyes should be.
"Keep well," she tells them, crawling into bed,
to dream whatever she will dream in that lovely haunted head.

CORONADO HEIGHTS

For Gretchen Hock

It little matters now
whether Coronado stood here on this hill
and accepted what is the general nature of things:
that there are no cities of gold, any more than there are
pots of the glittering stuff at the end of any rainbow,
for Coronado is four centuries of cold earth and bone.

What matters is the girl-woman beside me
whose hair is gold in this thin October sun,
whose eyes are blue with belief
when she says that one day she hopes
to bring her children here.

With a deep and wonder-struck heart
I, with less claim on her than father or lover,
hammer out a prayer for this precious girl,
whose face is as perfect as the song
the wind sings past the stones of this old castle:
that she love and be loved long and well,
that the horrors of this life pass her by,
that she grow graceful with age
and lose neither spirit nor mirth,
but prove in deed and thought
what is right and proper
for any goddess assigned to this earth.

THE WOMAN AND BLOOD

He nicks himself with a pocketknife
and wonders that she takes it so lightly,
turning from the dishes
to hand him a paper towel.
"Do you think I need stitches?"
The blood branches along his finger
like little red rivers headed for the sea.
"No," she says, returning to the sink.
"Clamp it tight and the bleeding will stop,
the flesh will knit. You'll heal."
"But the blood," he says, pressing the paper sleeve
around his finger and holding it out for her to see
like a little boy wounded at play.
"Yes, the blood," she says, smiling.
"You men bleed so seldom in your lives
and then from foolishness or fighting.
Men know so little of blood."
He watches her, this creature he loves,
mother of his children,
who knows blood the way he never can,
the secret and the surface,
the crust and the sacred wine,
moved by the seasons and the moon.
He bears his little pain, turns to his affairs,
finger throbbing, napkin stained.

THE LEOPARD MUSES ON HIS SPOTS

I cannot change them,
I am told by you people
who apply the rule of leopards
to the two-legged ape
who fancies himself better
than those who go about on four.

Why would I wish to change them,
though they do little to blend
me to the gray walls of my cage?
I am not gifted to ask
myself or others what a spot is
or what a spot is not
We are given what we have
and left with what we've got.

REDNECK WITH HAIR ON HIS BACK

Denton, Texas, 1990

Standing here in his muscle shirt at the bar,
with hair on his back and chest
and tufted like the stuff of nests
in opposing crotches of a too familiar tree,
he is little more than an upright ape
who has learned the alphabet.
With his woman he is not gentle,
preferring her in her anxious state,
taking her when he will,
and the children fear his thundering voice.

This, God's finest creation,
whose eyebrows now have drifted from his cheekbones
like continents over time until he sees clearly
between them with his dark eyes
and reasons well behind them
in that smoking vault of the brain,
where he knows what women are made for
and when to come in from the rain.

THE OLD GAME: BOY IN TRAINING

With glove and ball or pads and helmet
he trains for the day when in dark forest
or on the smoking field, facing
tooth and claw or enemy armed with steel
he will dash, as he must by ancient law,
into the way of harm and do his duty,
for what moves him is in the blood
engendered by a deeper urgency
than his father's wishes for him.

It matters not that meat now lies sealed
in cellophane at the supermarket,
that the frailest of girls may seize it,
that battles are fought with buttons
from a distant room. For he is *boy*,
man in the making, weapon for shaping,
and must be molded for the hunt or for war.

HE SPINS HIS TIRES

This is the only way that cars will go,
vroom, vroom, he races the engine and squalls
out onto the highway, burning Daddy's rubber.
Once it was the wind in his face,
his feet on sand or grass or stone,
chest thrust out, nostrils flared,
hair trailing flat out behind,
then atop a roaring horse, his heels
driving him faster, dust boiling
from four hammering hooves,
for he is *boy*, built for speed,
for running things down or over
or running from something,
a force like the wind itself,
cursed to be motion forever.

IV.
New Poems (2009)

Larry the Lawn Chair Man

All his life long he dreamed of flying,
and had he lived in a classical time
he would have fashioned his own wings
of feathers and wax and flown toward the sun,
so swept up in his ecstasy he would not have noticed
when the wax began to melt, feathers loosening,
would not have cared had he crashed into the sea,
his life complete, all that he had lived for.

On a day in his San Pedro backyard,
far from the classical world he yearned for,
he sat strapped in a Sears lawn chair,
forty-two weather balloons straining to lift him.
With sandwiches on board, beverages, and parachute,
CD radio, and BB gun to pop the balloons and descend,
he cut the rope that tethered him to his Jeep
and sprang up like a creature tired of gravity
and eager to ascend to the heavens, far above
the astonished crowd who watched him rise,
above the smoggy air and yapping dogs,
the screaming children, the news of the day.
He rose in wonder to over 16,000 feet,
the air so thin he could barely breathe,
so cold it felt like fire in his nose and throat,
drifted across to Long Beach, watched jets
zip over, under, and around him,
marveled at the many splendored earth
that lay below, the long curve of the sea,
the blue eyeball that stared up at him.

(continues)

In time he floated back over land,
felt that he had done what he had wanted to,
and started popping his balloons, one by one.
Forty-five minutes after he rose to the skies,
Larry fell into some power lines,
came to rest with throngs of well-wishers
about him, yapping dogs, screaming children.
He had returned to the earth that bore him.

But, ah, the rest of his life he remembered
the day he defied that terrible pull of gravity.
In dark and light he dreamed of floating above it all,
breathing deep the thin air that burned his lungs,
watched the sea crawl toward the teeming shore,
a vast mesh of buildings, power lines, and roads.
He dreamed of building another craft,
with a larger chair and more balloons.
He dreamed of hovering near the sun.

Alas, he never flew again, accepting
the absence of wings, bowing to the tug of earth.
In the Angeles National Forest Larry Walters
put a bullet through his heart, suffered his final fall,
victim of the awful law of gravity,
the heavy force that will take us all.

Eagle Girl

High in the weather-smitten crags they found her,
huddled in a nest littered with small bones.
And when they tried to rescue her,
they were set upon by three eagles
and the eagle girl herself,
slashing with talon-like fingernails.

But at last they subdued her
and took her to a remote cabin
for extensive observation
by a person skilled in such matters.

At last report, she seemed no nearer
to being a human female child
than when she was taken from the nest.
The psychologist noted the following:
That she is terrified of humans,
sleeps perched on a bookshelf,
preens herself as if she had feathers,
pounces on mice and eats them alive,
flaps her arms in imitation of flight.
In short, she is not ready for school
or church or shopping at Wal-Mart
and would make a poor companion
for others of her ilk and age.

Meanwhile those who care for her
sit anguished, pondering what to do,
whether to establish a college fund
or admit her to the circus or the zoo.

WHEN THE MUMMY BECAME A MOMMY

Unearthed by workers at a Cairo site,
weeks she lay coated with sepia dust
in the back room of a city museum
in dark and silence and solitude,
patience a key virtue for the long-dead.

When he came the first time, he slipped in,
propped his broom and mop in a corner,
pulled up a chair, sat long and studied
in the pale glow of his flashlight beam
her thin and wraith-like figure,
wondering what lay beneath the windings.
Then he came again, bringing candles,
lighting them, placing them at either end
of the case they had her stretched out in.
In time, he touched her ancient wrappings.
Now fingers were where they shouldn't be,
his feverish hands stroked her length.
He sang soft tunes of love, and
in the silence of that lonely room
rose whispers and sounds of passion.

Months later someone discovered
her carelessly rewrapped body
and noted her bulging belly.
A doctor found a heartbeat,
determined that she was pregnant.

Dobi Sitar his name was, the man
who fell for this ancient creature,
resurrected her with passionate love
after 3000 years of dreamless sleep.
Dobi laid aside his mop and broom
and ended up in prison to lie upon his bunk
day after day, studying the gray ceiling,
enduring the scathing ridicule of many,
including the prison cooks, whose joke
was a special dish for him, Necrafiligumbo.

(continues)

Meanwhile, the mummy became a mommy,
baby removed by Tut-Cut Section.
Baby is well and waiting for adoption.
Mommy is a cold, silent mummy again.
Rewrapped and tucked in cozy,
she is propped up now for all to view,
lying under glass and colorful lights,
dreamless and loveless and mute.

WHY AMELIA WENT DOWN

*The following poetic interpretation of the last flight of Amelia Earhart is
based upon notes found in the remains of a briefcase belonging to Fred
Noonan, her navigator. He managed to scribble some final notes before they
crashed. I have no reason to doubt the authority of this material, since it
was reported in the* Weekly World News, *a highly reputable source in these
days of relaxed journalism.*

They bounced down the dusty runway,
gathered speed, and rose that final time,
their shadow sliding over jungle trees,
bellies full of New Guinea Thunder Beans.
Another leg of the journey lay before them:
a routine flight to Howland Island,
where an anchored Coast Guard cutter
lay loaded with fuel and supplies.
She was intent behind the yoke,
eyes ever on the instruments before her,
adjusting altitude and speed, noting the
pressure of the oil, the rpm of the engines.
Beside her Noonan plotted the course,
a lapboard on his briefcase, marked
point after point on the line he had drawn
to the place that they were going.

And then, oh then, the rumble of nearby thunder...

She was first, grimacing long minutes
before yielding to biological urge.
She would not meet his eyes, so
Noonan could only sit and wonder.
Then she rotated in her seat, raised one hip,
the one away from Noonan, and filled
the cabin with the gas of Thunder Beans.
He knew then the reason for their name.

(continues)

Noonan held hard his breath and
scribbled as he watched her writhe,
noted her clenched teeth, her rolling eyes,
her hands clawing at the window latch.
There had been no sound above the engines,
but well he knew the reason for her anguish.
And then he felt his own near thunder
begin deep in his bowels, burgeon
like a July storm, the great boiling cloud
seeking an exit, more room in the cockpit
than there was in his belly and gut.
When Noonan erupted, it was like a smell from hell,
he wrote, as vile as hers or worse.
He swept his eyes across the panel,
and the instruments were a shapeless shimmer.
Amelia huddled, a ghostlike figure,
head thrust from the window
to draw in precious air, still
blasting the gas of Thunder Beans
at poor Noonan, who could hold
his breath no longer. He yanked
at the window on his side until he
could hang his head into the slipstream
and gulp a different kind of wind.

When at last he withdrew his head,
his eyes now free of tears and focused,
Amelia was staring at him, eyes glazed over,
her mouth full open but full as well.
He could see the tips of wings, feathers of a tail,
and two tiny feet draped across her lower lip.
The plane by now had slid well off-course,
banking hard to the left and losing altitude.
In those few seconds as they fell,
Noonan wrote fast in his journal:
"My darling Amelia has swallowed a gull.
We are going down. Goodbye cruel world."

And so the story of Amelia Earhart and her fated flight
is removed from the ponderous book of mystery
and assigned its place in the pages of simple history.

A GLIMPSE OF THE STONE AGE, ACCORDING TO MACK DRYDEN

My friend Mack Dryden, former trailer- and housemate at
Southern Mississippi, is now a motivational speaker, comedian,
and movie star out on the Left Coast, but married and with kids and,
from all I can tell, fairly normal for someone living in California, albeit
he does kill squirrels in his yard and uses them in gumbo. Much of
my deeper understanding of history comes from him.

Seems it couldn't be more than a millennium or so,
but this month marks the 100,000th anniversary
of the beginning of The Stone Age,
billed by its Neanderthal organizers as
Sixty Thousand Years of Peace and Music and Mud.

Like most other great eras, this one began humbly,
even by Paleolithic standards.
One day, a few long-haired elders
(you made elder at 19 back then,
when most medical treatment involved
a scary-looking guy dancing around shaking bones)
were sitting around, gnawing on bear meat,
discussing who would be Lunch Bait the next day,
when someone threw a bunch of hemp on the fire,
and gradually the conversation turned whimsical.

After noting the amazing brilliance of the marmalade skies,
one free-thinker had a notion: What if they threw an Age,
and everybody went naked, sloshed around in the mud,
smoked and ingested anything they wanted to,
and did the Fido-style boogaloo whenever,
wherever, and with whomever they desired?

The group thought it was a grand idea
and celebrated by eating everything in a two-mile strip.

(continues)

The Stone Age (not to be confused with The Rock Era)
was named, of course, for the single ingredient
found in most durable goods of the period:
versatile and attractive stone, which was waterproof,
shock-resistant, and, most importantly, everywhere,
therefore making rock cartels impractical.
And, true to its long-lasting namesake,
The Stone Age had a dazzling 60,000-year run for obvious reasons:
One, if you ate a plant that enabled you to see a girl
with kaleidoscope eyes or even The Walrus,
you could just sit back and enjoy it
without fear of a surprise blood test at work
or cops knocking at the mouth of the cave.
(*Downside: if the ivory-tusked Walrus
you were grinning back at happened
in fact to be a saber-toothed tiger,
you probably wouldn't be evolving
with the rest of the group.)

Two, when musicians started pounding
those hollow logs and howling,
you could get naked and dance in the mud
'til the mammoths came home,
and nobody hassled you as long
as you didn't sing louder than the band.
(*Downside: drum solos sometimes lasted for weeks.)

Three, if you saw a fetching lass bending over,
gathering berries, you didn't even have to say,
"Excuse me, do you come to this flood plain often?"
before contributing your brow ridge to the gene pool.
(*Downside for the ladies: Back then, every gentleman caller was,
well, a Neanderthal, so if you weren't into chinless guys
with thick skulls and sloping foreheads
and a tendency to relieve themselves by the fire,
you either had to lower your standards,
stay home every weekend, or wait for The Neolithic Age.)

(continues)

Four, incredible feasts grew on trees and wandered
around in herds, and the portions were huge.
(*Downside: Some creatures had not yet
gotten the word that Man was atop the food chain,
so exactly who would comprise the Dinner Special
was often decided only after a loud and ugly scene.
Also, handling fire was still an iffy proposition,
so if you were picky, you could starve to death waiting
around for lightning to render your buffalo, say, medium well.)

Everything has to come to an end, of course,
and this party was no exception.
Even the most venerable traditions—
dancing naked, being filthy and semi-conscious,
mating with the most human-looking mud lumps
at the campsite—began to lose their novelty.

Eventually there were only a few old people
sitting around talking about how great things were
during The Good Old Age, before this fancy Bronze
business started. How things were made to last back then,
because their knives and spearheads and garlic presses
and weed whackers were made out of real rock,
the way the gods intended, not like this sissy stuff we use today.

And the music back then! Whoa!
Now that was the real thing:
Hard-driving, big-beat, whoop-and-holler music,
not this sappy flute and harp stuff you can't even dance to.

So when somebody gets nostalgic for the Good Old Age
and decides to throw a 100,000th Anniversary Stone Age Celebration,
it'll no doubt result in a pale facsimile.
Hell, they'll probably even charge you to get in.
[*Mack, by the way, says that he missed Woodstock himself,
being from Mississippi, where the sixties arrived in June of 1977.*]

In 999 Erikson Sailed the Ocean Brine...The Discovery

The story actually began in 960,
when the great Norse explorer Erik the Red
sailed off to find a warm island paradise
and instead discovered Iceland,
where summer usually comes and goes
on the second Thursday of July.

Erik's first mate, Oscar the Orange,
suggested they go find Hawaii or the Bahamas—
someplace they didn't have to wear fur coats to the beach—
but Erik said those places were for sissy explorers
like Bjorn the Beige and Lars the Lavender.

So he sailed off again and found another humongous island,
which he named Greenland, hoping his men wouldn't notice
that it was just as cold and miserable as Iceland.

Soon, however, his men realized that Greenland
was actually named for the color your toes turn
before you have to leave them on the tundra
(from the Norse: *tun*, or "God-forsaken," and *dra*, "hell-hole").

After Erik retired, with the traditional granite and pewter sundial,
his son Leif (pronounced "Leif") changed his name from "The Red"
to "Erik's Son" for credit purposes, later dropped the apostrophe
because it was tacky, and became Leif Erikson,
Unsung Real Discoverer of the New World.

Young Leif carried on his father's lifetime quest to find
the most uncomfortable places on earth.
Finally, after untold hardships, he Found a New Land
he called New Found Land, all the creative types
having frozen to death during the crossing
(thus saving us an early infestation of poets, you see).

(continues)

So, in 999, over 400 years before Christopher Columbus
was a nauseous look in his mother's eye,
Erikson rode the boat ashore, Hallelujah,
and set foot on the New World.

As the discoverer of a Brand New Place,
Erikson had a duty to spread disease, loot the land,
and enslave the native populations.
(He studied the same books on exploring that Chris did.)
He was thus disappointed to find that Newfoundland
contained not a single peace-loving population to enslave
(or slaughter, if the fun got rough).
Deeming the rape and pillage prospects limited at best
(some experts cite a species of red-bearded moose
in Eastern Canada as evidence that at least some interaction occurred),
Erikson ordered his men to dig a few foundations
and scatter around some stuff that could later be carbon-dated.

Then, certain that he would have a bank holiday
or at the very least a city in Ohio or Mississippi named after him,
Erikson left the New World and returned triumphantly
to the Previously-Owned World, having secured his place
in history as an annoying asterisk that would one day
drive American History purists stark-raving, betsy-bug crazy.

[You can imagine what it was like living two years
in the presence of such knowledge,
an intellectually-starved Plato tugging at the robe
of my own Socrates, who preferred Boone's Farm apple wine
to hemlock—thank you, Jesus. Gladly did I learn,
and over the years to come, gladly did I teach.]

TO an uncommon prostitute

I have never met you,
was always afraid the woman I was with
would not understand. Why would she?
In New Orleans once I tried with a twenty
to buy an hour of time with you,
not to join my body with you
but rather my mind,
you, the oldest comfort
man has had
to address his many needs,
whether in a sweaty bed,
his nostrils filled with the smell of you
or quietly at opposite ends of a couch
in some strange room
where in words soft and low
he tells you what his life has become,
asks you what he should do
to understand a woman
he has loved but is close to losing.
Asks you as a boy might
to understand how to
touch the bright creature
across the room from him,
a girl whose face he worshipped
for long years before he knew
the deep, dark secrets of her.
How do you see yourself,
neither mother nor wife nor lover,
when this crippled soul empties itself
before you, weeps in your arms?
Are you whore now, that word
so filthy on the tongue?
Or are you, bathed in an angelic glow,
a message from the God of all lost men,
designed to listen in some dark room,
to whisper, to touch, and to understand?

DIVER OFF FLORIDA COAST SEXUALLY ASSAULTED BY 300-POUND TURTLE

When he descended on her,
it was like a dark cloud, she said,
blotting out the light from above,
and then he was pressing her
into the very sand itself,
rolling her in the waving grass
that grew along the bottom.
"I could not determine what it was
at first, nor decide its full intentions."
Was he protecting his mate or patch
of seaweed she was swimming through?

Scratched and mewling like a baby,
she stands at the edge of the surf
staring out over the glassy water.
"He touched me with his thing," she says,
"and that was when I finally knew
what he was after. I tried as hard as I could
to squirm out from under that hard belly."

But a turtle of that magnitude,
once he has you in his grasp,
is not easily denied.
He continued to press and probe
until she yanked her hose away
and thrust the stream of bubbles
into his slitted eyes, whereupon
he relented and let her go.

(continues)

Still she stands at the edge of the ocean,
shaken to the core by that deep encounter,
eyes fixed on the bulge of water before her,
thinking how like a giant turtle's back it looks,
thinking how lying beneath a giant turtle feels,
trapped between those hard plates,
the flailing legs slashing at her,
and the grassy soft sea floor below,
in that most unnatural of events
when the human and the beast
struggle to fulfill a burning desire
for what Nature says they must have,
as mythic as the ancient earth itself,
as real as the sand, the sea, the air.

EATING CHICKEN BACKS

Go to any fast-food place these days
this side of distant Biafra
and ask for a whole fried chicken.
In the bucket or bag you will find
eight pieces, four matching sets:
wings, drumsticks, thighs, and breasts,
with the center-line, the main beam,
that which holds the other parts together,
missing as surely as neck, head and feet.
Assemble those eight pieces however you will
and what you have will be far less than a chicken:
some ill-concocted hybrid more fit
for a freak show than for the table.

Once upon my youth, when Mother fried a chicken,
all would be on the platter but head and feet
and innards, but for liver and gizzard,
which my father insisted on.
While others argued over drumstick and thigh,
screamed out for the lucky wishbone,
I went straight for the pieces of back,
where the tastiest morsels of chicken lay.

Alas, the lowly back has fallen out of favor,
poor dirty cousins of chicken anatomy,
fit to season a stew maybe
or make broth or giblet gravy.
Mid-line pieces, amorphous,
with not enough meat to keep a man alive
If he ate them 'round the clock.
They have faded into the culinary past.

Ah, but the supermarket still sells
the whole chicken, sans neck, head, and feet,
and you may hack out your own back,
batter it up, fry it, and enjoy.

(continues)

A caveat: Never attempt to eat a back
with fork and knife upon your plate.
It cannot be done with finesse
or any degree of reasonable success.
You must seize it with both hands
and attack it like a savage,
grappling, rotating, gnawing,
the scrumptious flesh moist and richer
by far than any taste you'd find
heaped in the striped bucket.
Grease dribbling down your arms,
crust speckling table and floor,
you are lost in your own savory heaven.
While others point and leer,
the primitive depths of you
declare that in anybody's jungle
you are the winner here.

When at last the Judgment comes,
our modern chicken halves,
robbed of that which makes them whole,
will leaves their shelves and trays, hobble off
to whatever heaven they go to,
leg bone to thigh bone to wing to breast,
cobbled together for eternity, unable to walk
or squawk or to roost upon a nest.

ACKNOWLEDGMENTS

Poems from *Lighting the Furnace Pilot* reprinted with permission of Spoon River Poetry Press.

Poems from *Circling* reprinted with permission of Browder Springs Press.

Poems from *The Book of Boys and Girls* reprinted with permission of Louisiana Literature Press

"Eagle Girl" and "When the Mommy Became a Mummy" initially appeared in *Boulevard*.

ABOUT THE AUTHOR

Paul Ruffin, Texas State University System Regents' Professor and Distinguished Professor of English at Sam Houston State University, is the founding editor of *The Texas Review* and founding director of Texas Review Press. He is the author of two novels, three collections of short stories, two books of essays, and six earlier collections of poetry. He is also a newspaper columnist and feature writer.

Poems in this collection have appeared widely in journals in this country, including *Poetry*, *Paris Review*, *Southern Review*, *Georgia Review*, *Michigan Quarterly Review*, etc.

Readers are invited to visit Ruffin at http://pauldruffin.com.

PAUL RUFFIN
NEW AND SELECTED POEMS

ISBN 978-0-87565-409-6

Case. $15.95

TCU TEXAS POETS LAUREATE SERIES

ISBN 978-0-87565-409-6

9 780875 654096

51595